Locomotives of the London Midland and Scottish Railway

Written by Alan Bloom
Compiled by David Williams

It was obvious that drastic reorganisation of the Railways was needed
World War. During that war, all the Rail
under centralised government control.
Parliament made Grouping possible. It
Geddes, who had been a railwayman b
which set amalgamation as the aim. No
integration into one system; the idea slow
companies should join together into four
other. Such a step was rational, not only f
with harmful rivalries, the overlapping of i … a generally better service, both passenger and freight. Some companies were close to becoming bankrupt, and though railway shares had mostly been safe and sometimes profitable, there were danger signals ahead.

It took a year of consultation and discussion to decide which companies would be best welded together. Some resented the idea of losing their identity by being absorbed by a larger neighbour, whilst the latter were all the more intent on domination. Two of the largest companies, the London & North Western and the Midland, had been on less-than-friendly terms for years but now they had no option but to unite, along with many lesser lines, as the London, Midland & Scottish. As a group it encompassed such far away places as Poole in Dorset and Wick in the far north of Scotland, with four termini in London, at Euston, St Pancras, Broad Street and Fenchurch Street. It was easily the largest of the four groups formed in 1922–3, with a network of close on 10,000 route miles. No longer could the L.N.W.R. call

Front cover Stanier pacific No. 46238 'City of Carlisle' is off the beaten track, standing in Skipton Station on 27 September 1963. She is waiting to take over a RCTS-SLS special train for the run over Ais Gill summit to her home city. (*John Warr*)

Back cover Nineteenth-century Johnson IF 0–6–0 tank No. 41835 shunts at Staveley ironworks in 1962. These ancient locomotives became the last survivors of their type, being provided by British Rail under an old agreement to shunt the works. They were maintained at Staveley (Barrow Hill) depot. (*Allan Preston*)

Right: The view from the fireman's side of LMSR Stanier pacific No. 46245 *City of London* at Crewe on 1 September 1964. A coveted position for enthusiasts to occupy, and a view that a pacific fireman had very little time to appreciate, such was the size of the firebox. (*Derek Tuck*)

itself with pride, 'The Premier Line', or the Midland reply with its slogan, 'The Best Way'!

The following were the principal companies absorbed in the new system:

Company	*Total stock*	*Principal works*
London & North Western	3,336 locomotives	Crewe
Midland	3,019 locomotives	Derby
Lancashire & Yorkshire	1,650 locomotives	Horwich
Caledonian	1,072 locomotives	St Rollox (Glasgow)
Glasgow & South Western	528 locomotives	Kilmarnock

The total is massive even without those belonging to several smaller companies. The latter often had their engines built either by the larger companies, or by outside independent builders. But the L.M.S. was now the largest transport system in the world, with a larger work force than any other concern, and it was finding itself unwieldy, as if unable to tackle its vast responsibilities. There were several reasons why the bemused giant failed to get to grips with its task, and one of these must have been because of the multiplicity of engine types. Of these, there were well over a hundred, which is not very surprising, having absorbed so many companies, most of which had engine classes built by successive designers. The work of at least twenty-five designers (now known as Chief Mechanical Engineers) was represented.

Some locomotives, then still in service, dated back to the 1860s or 1870s when first

Below: A scene at Birmingham's New Street Station that will evoke memories for many train spotters. On the right of the view, Stanier Class 5 No. 44893 of Newton Heath is about to head the 10.00 to Leeds, and on the left Fowler 4F 0–6–0 No. 43949 of Saltley has just brought in the 07.30 local from Gloucester. 10.08, 26 June 1960. (*Michael Mensing*)

Right: The London and North Western possessed the largest number of locomotives of the constituents of the LMS. Their Precedent 2–4–0 No. 790 *Hardwicke* of 1892 was used in the 'Railway Race to the North' in 1895, and covered the 141 miles from Crewe to Carlisle at an average of nearly 70 mph.

Now part of the National Railway Museum collection, it is seen at the Rail 150 celebration at Shildon, on 31 August 1975. (*D. C. Williams*)

Centre Right: A more lasting reminder of the LNWR was Bowen Cooke's 0–8–0 of 1901. Counting minor variations, just over 500 were built, and 200 survived into the sixties. Super D No. 49430 is illustrated at their last operational depot, Bescot (Walsall). (*Allan Preston*)

Bottom Right: The main locomotive workshops for the LNWR were at Crewe. Here LMS Stanier 8F 2–8–0 No. 48351 is undergoing repair on 19 September 1964. (*Derek Tuck*)

built, though when rebuilds occurred, variations in design were mostly the rule. The L.N.W.R. versus Midland rivalry had produced somewhat distinctive policies. For example, the former preferred large engines, while the latter believed in smaller, lighter ones, even if it meant, as frequently happened, double-heading on express trains whenever the load exceeded a prescribed tonnage. Under the enforced amalgamation the Midland fought hard to inject some of its policies into the L.M.S. and the livery adopted for passenger engines was a red very close to its own, the L.N.W.R. having been black. More important was that its C.M.E., Henry Fowler, filled the same position on the newly-enlarged system from 1925. He had taken over, just as Hughes had done when the Lancashire & Yorkshire Railway merged with the L.N.W.R. in 1921. He thus became overlord on locomotive design for the future.

In 1923, the era of large passenger locomotives had only just begun, and despite the long routes from Euston and St Pancras the L.M.S. had nothing larger than the 4–6–0 'Claughtons'. These had, over about twenty years, come in for considerable modification and rebuilding but despite some being four-cylindered, none were heavier than 79 tons (without tender) with a working pressure of only 180 lb/in.^{2}; these were L.N.W.R. engines, but the Midland had nothing larger than the 4–4–0 Compounds, of not much over 60 tons. Compounding was, by the way, not widely

Above, a splendid example of Midland Railway restoration; Midland Compound 4P 4–4–0 No. 1000, built at Derby in 1902, is here seen on a Railway Correspondence and Travel Society special from Nottingham to Swindon at Rugby Central on 11 September 1960. The station, on the erstwhile Great Central main line, was alien territory for the Midland Railway locomotive. (*Derek Smith*)
Top Right: Some of these Midland Railway 2F 0–6–0s were still in use in the 1960s, the last survivors of over 170 locomotives. No. 58166 was photographed at Coalville, Leicester-

shire, where their diminutive size allowed them to negotiate Glenfield tunnel on the Leicester West Bridge branch, 1962. (*John Warr*)

Centre Right: The 4F 0–6–0s were the last development of the basic design shown above; one of the examples, built in the Midland Railway days, No. 43924, heads a down semi-fitted freight through Widney Manor on the Great Western main line on 18 August 1959. This locomotive is now in use on the Worth Valley Railway. (*Michael Mensing*)

Bottom Right: The Midland Railway also produced a very

successful breed of 0–6–0 side tank, perpetuated into LMSR days with minor variations. Here No. 47228, one of a class of sixty locomotives introduced in 1899, is seen on Walton-on-the-Hill shed, Liverpool, in mid 1963, shortly before both depot and locomotives were liquidated. The locomotive retains the condensing gear from London area underground duties. (*Allan Preston*)

Above: The Lancashire and Yorkshire Railway operated a large fleet of 0–6–0 tender engines, the smallest and earliest of these being the 'Ironclads' of 1887. With an engine weight of thirty-nine tons and boiler pressure 140 lb/in.² they were – by later standards – primitive machines. Withdrawn from Wakefield in 1959, No. 52044 was the last survivor of fifty engines. It is here seen crossing Mytholmes Viaduct on the Worth Valley Railway on 2 August 1977, during a 'Ninetieth Birthday' steaming. (*J. G. Mallinson*)

Bottom Left: The Worth Valley Railway is foremost in the preservation of locomotives of the Lancashire and Yorkshire Railway. No. 51218 only survivor of a class of fifty-seven 0–4–0 saddle tanks built from 1891 onwards, is seen on display at the Rail 150 celebrations at Shildon, Co. Durham on 31 August 1975. These diminutive locomotives weighed only twenty-one tons, and were to be seen in dockland areas from Liverpool in the west to Goole in the east. After 1923, the LMS extended their areas of operation, and British Rail even more so. They were frequently loaned to private concerns when private locomotives were under repair. (*D. C. Williams*)

Right: Most Somerset and Dorset Railway locomotives were of pure Midland Railway design. The ten 2–8–0 tender locomotives first introduced in 1914 were however specially designed for that hilly railway and were an undoubted success over the now closed seventy-one miles from Bath to Bournemouth. The class became extinct on British Rail in 1964, though two examples languished at Barry scrapyard and are now in course of restoration for West Somerset Railway and North Yorkshire Moors Railway service. Here British Rail 7F No. 53806 prepares to leave Bath Green Park for Bristol with an empty pigeon special on 19 August 1963. (*Michael Hale*)

practised in Britain, though it appeared to make sense for steam to pass first to one cylinder and on to the second before being exhausted through the chimney. They were, none the less, smart engines and as with all Midland rolling stock were maintained in spanking condition and appearance.

With the Great Western four-cylinder 'Castle' Class 4–6–0s and Gresley's three-cylinder 4–6–2 Pacifics coming into service in 1923, the L.M.S. was dropping behind. The need to catch up was obvious and urgent, and yet under George Hughes very little was done beyond smartening up existing engines. Sir Henry Fowler took over as C.M.E. in 1925, and in 1927 brought out the 4–6–0 *Royal Scot*. Though to a large extent it was a development from the earlier 'Claughton,' it weighed 84 tons without tender, but both boiler pressure and tractive effort were much higher. Many were, however, rebuilt in later years replacing the parallel boiler with a tapered one, and replacing the original tiny chimney with a large one to take a double blastpipe.

The Walschaerts valve gear was now becoming widely used on both the L.M.S. and L.N.E.R. It was a Belgian invention and the basic 'Stephenson motion' which had reigned for so long was disappearing except for inside-cylindered locomotives, only the Great Western still favouring the latter. The Belpaire-style firebox – with its wide top exceeding the width of the boiler barrel – was also more often seen, and the value of superheating was being generally accepted. This reduced the number of small boiler tubes – usually $1\frac{3}{4}$ in. diameter – by about half. The upper half of the boiler tubeplate was fitted with thirty to forty flue tubes of about 5 in. diameter, and through these a cluster of quite small tubes was inserted. These were the superheaters. Steam from the boiler passed through them and with the hottest of the fire gases surrounding them, raised the steam temperature – and likewise the power – still higher. From the superheater headers steam then passed down to the cylinders.

Royal Scot had a working pressure of 200 lb/in.^{2} and with 6 ft 9 in. driving wheels resulted in a tractive effort fifty per cent greater than any other L.M.S. engine. Though still lagging a little in power compared with the L.N.E.R. under Gresley, Sir Henry Fowler had in *Royal Scot* a basic design which was to stand the L.M.S. in good stead later on. There was, however, little scope so far for standardisation, except on main line running. Beyond the Border into Scotland, designs tended to perpetuate those already in existence, for on such a vast network there were limitations in many areas; in weight, speed and wheel arrangement. Many of the oldest engines were scrapped, as new building brought replacements, but since the L.M.S. served several large industrial and mining areas, the need for keeping up freight standards had also to be met. The ubiquitous 0–6–0, many of which dated from Victorian times, formed a large part of L.M.S. total motive power. These, along with tank engines of many types from 0–4–0 to 4–6–2 and even up to 0–8–4, far exceeded in numbers the larger, more attractive-looking express passenger locomotives.

One of the most handsome of the smaller passenger engines was the Midland

2–4–0. These were first built by Kirtley in the 1860s and continued by Johnson up to the 1880s. With large diameter driving wheels, but very little protection for the crew, they were simple and speedy, weighing only 40 tons, and with double-heading were used on the expresses as well as local routes. As rebuilds, they were still in service until the 1920s and 30s, outliving some of the larger, more recently built, 'Precursors' and 'Claughtons' of the L.N.W.R. section.

Despite the depression of the late 1920s and dwindling profitability, the four main L.M.S. locomotive works of Crewe, Derby, Horwich and St Rollox (Glasgow) were not ideal; indeed, the first batch of fifty 'Royal Scots' was built by an outside firm – the North British Locomotive Co. Ltd. of Glasgow. The need for greater power for coal traffic also brought interest in the articulated Garratt invention, built by Beyer Peacock of Gorton, Manchester. These were already being exported overseas in increasing numbers, for they were virtually double engines. The boiler was suspended between two tenders, each having the same set of cylinders and motion as on a conventional engine. But only one (hard working) crew was needed, for boiler steam passed to the cylinders through a flexible pipe. Their own fuel consumption was heavy, but they could pull 1,200-ton coal trains from the Toton marshalling yards near Nottingham to the London distribution centre at Cricklewood without much trouble. They were not, however, very popular with engine crews in spite of doing good service, and not even the rotating coal

Below: Few locomotives were finished more ornately than Caledonian Railway locomotives. 4–2–2 No. 123 took part in the first race to the North in 1888 having been built by Neilsons of Glasgow in 1886. As LMS No. 14010, the locomotive was saved for preservation by that company in 1935. From 1958 until 1965 the locomotive was activated for running special trains, mainly in Scotland. This view was taken at the still extant Carstairs Station on 19 April 1965. (*David Idle*)

Right: The Caledonian Railway Pickersgill 4–4–0s, built between 1916 and 1922, were a well-known part of the Scottish

scene until the early 1960s. No. 54485 was one of the last survivors and is here seen waiting to leave the north end of Perth Station with an enthusiasts special to Methven on 15 June 1960. (*John Warr*)

Bottom Right: Over two hundred of the Caledonian 2F 0–6–0s (nicknamed Jumbo's) were in use from their inception in 1883 until 1963. In this scene railway enthusiasts were riding in the wagons of a freight at Millisle, on the Whithorn branch in Galloway, on 15 April 1963. No. 57375 was allocated to Stranraer depot at the time, and withdrawn a few months later. (*David Idle*)

bunkers with which most were later fitted saved them from ultimate extinction in Britain. Only one small 0–4–0+0–4–0 Garratt is preserved in England at Bressingham, though many are still in service in Africa.

With these outsiders should be mentioned the Midland banking engine, nicknamed 'Big Bertha'. This was designed to assist trains up the two-mile Lickey Incline of 1 in 37, and with its 0–10–0 wheel arrangement below a very large boiler, and an engine-only weight of 73½ tons, it had, until the Garratts came, the highest tractive effort rating of any engine in Britain; over 43,000 lb.

After the first few years of relative muddle and inaction, the years 1926 to 1930 brought evidence of progress towards standardisation of design. Only thirty-eight engines of the pre-Grouping designs were built, and these were eighteen of the Caledonian 4–6–0s, and twenty more 4–4–2 'Tilbury' tanks. These were for the short run on the London, Tilbury & Southend Railway, operating from Fenchurch Street Station and with workshops at Plaistow. It was an independent company until 1912 when the Midland directors bought it from under the nose of the Great Eastern, to which geographically it should have belonged. The 'Tilburys' were handsome engines, well kept in their apple-green livery and named after stations on their route – of which *Thundersley* remains preserved. The building to the new L.M.S. standard accounted for 1,382 engines in the years 1926–30 – with a

noticeable drop in the last of those years, due no doubt to the Depression. Totals varied considerably amongst the twelve classes – including tank versions of some, and the thirty-eight Garratts. More than half the total were 0–6–0s, the Class 3 and 4 freight engines. The latter was a plain but typical design with inside cylinders giving them a top-heavy appearance applicable to many other 0–6–0s when large boilers were placed high up on a fairly short wheelbase. These and the slightly smaller Class 3 joined the hundreds of older designs already in service, working freight trains over the whole system, with Class 7 0–8–0s for heavier mineral trains.

The 'mixed traffic' concept was introduced during this period. There were advantages in having dual-purpose engines, for when the need arose for economy, a return to base shed could be achieved by switching from passenger to freight and vice versa, rather than running home 'light'. The 2–6–0 Horwich-built Class 5 ('Crab'), of which 225 were built during those five years, filled such a need. It also indicated features in design which were to remain largely unchanged until the last days of steam, which are apparent when compared with the B.R. Standard Class 4, built twenty-five years later.

Although nothing larger in tank engines than the Class 4 2–6–4 was built in the late 1920s, this had become a standard design calling for far more than the seventy-three new ones built during the period. The system already had some large 4–6–4 'Baltic' tanks, taken over from the Furness and Glasgow & South Western Railways. The latter were to the design of Robert Whitelegg who, like his father before him, had been C.M.E. of the London Tilbury & Southend. He resented the Midland takeover, and went as C.M.E. for the G. & S.W., but when thwarted again by the 1923 Grouping, resigned from railway service and joined the firm of Beyer Peacock as General Manager at their Gorton works.

Sir Henry Fowler's reign ended in 1931. He left many achievements, including superheating and compounding, but also many frustrations. He wished to delve more deeply into compounding, but his proposals were not accepted, either for his 4–6–0 or 4–6–2. As a means of proving that the L.M.S. did not need a 4–6–2 Pacific, the loan of a Great Western 'Castle' had been arranged in 1926 much to Fowler's

Left: LMS 1925-built Midland Compound No. 41123 is coupled to a Jubilee 4–6–0 at Gloucester Eastgate Station on 28 March 1959. (*John Tarrant*)
Right: The Midland 2P 4–4–0 was slightly updated in 1928 for distribution over the whole LMS system. No. 40663 is seen at Elgin, north-east Scotland. (*John Warr*)
Below: Preserved Highland Railway Jones Goods 4–6–0 No. 103 of 1894, at Leeds Holbeck on 25 May 1964. It was returning to Scotland from Bedford after starring in 'Those Magnificent Men in Their Flying Machines'. Now resident in Glasgow Museum.
(*Gavin Morrison*)

R.C.T.S.-S.L.S.
NORTH EASTERN TOUR
1963
44467
44467

47396
47396

chagrin. The four-cylindered 4–6–0 *Launceston Castle*, with its high boiler pressure, made some outstanding runs, showing great efficiency and economy of fuel, and so diverted Fowler back to a 4–6–0, and the introduction of *Royal Scot* a year later.

After Ernest Lemon's brief stay, the Stanier regime began in 1932. William Stanier, later to be knighted, brought with him some Great Western ideas and ideals. But he was not content with a 4–6–0 for the strenuous Euston–Glasgow run. It was important to compete with Gresley and the King's Cross–Edinburgh route, for his A3 Pacifics had mastered the run to the extent of achieving non-stop running. The Executive Board headed by Sir Josiah Stamp (later Lord Stamp) had

Above: The Caledonian 0–4–4 tanks of class 439 were perpetuated into LMS days. One of the later examples, No. 55263, shunts empty stock at Oban during the evening of 18 May 1961. (*Michael Mensing*)

Above Left: The Midland Railway design of 4F 0–6–0 was built in large numbers in LMS days. No. 44467 was one of the last built, and is seen off native territory taking water at Wetherby during railtour working on 27 September 1963. (*John Warr*)

Left: LMS 3F 0–6–0 Standard Tank No. 47396, built in 1925 photographed at Arley colliery near Nuneaton on 18 September 1960. This type was multiplied to a total of over 400 examples. (*John Tarrant*)

Right: Another 3F 0–6–0 tank at work on shunting duties at Crewe carriage sidings. Many were in use there and at all other major LMS stations and yards, and nicknamed 'Jinties' by enthusiasts. No. 47450 was pictured on 31 December 1960. (*Derek Smith*)

Left: The only non-Midland design to be produced after the grouping was the Hughes 2–6–0, familiarly known as the 'Crab', of Lancashire and Yorkshire Railway Horwich origin. 245 examples were to be found on the LMS system on a wide variety of duties. Here No. 42900 of Saltley climbs the Lickey Incline with an untypically short train. (*John Tarrant*)

Left: Even in original parallel boiler form, the Fowler *Royal Scot* 4–6–0s were well liked amongst enginemen. Seventy examples were built between 1927 and 1930. No. 6152 *The Kings Dragoon Guardsman* pauses at Oxenholme with a northbound Anglo-Scottish express, in 1939. Ahead lie Grayrigg and Shap inclines. The design of these 4–6–0s owed much to the North British Locomotive Company.
(*D. J. Montgomery Collection*)

Left: Another outside contract was placed with Beyer Peacock for the supply of Garratt 2–6–0 + 0–6–2 articulated locomotives. Thirty-three were built, and they were usually to be found on Toton–Brent, Toton–Washwood Heath, and Chesterfield–York coal hauls. Here No. 47996 passes Water Orton Station Jcn, in July 1955. The LMS Garratts became extinct in 1958.
(*D. J. Montgomery Collection*)

Right: Fowler Class 4 2–6–4 tanks were built from 1927 onwards and the concept was successfully developed into the British Railways era. Here No. 42350 of Willesden depot halts at Wansford with 'The Fernie' railtour from Northampton on 25 August 1962. 125 of the locomotives were built, and supplanted only by dieselisation in the 1960s. They could be found on local passenger services over most of the LMS system, and also banking duties at certain places. (*John Warr*)

Below: Fowler 2–6–4 tank No. 42419 of Saltley enters the now closed Blackwell Station, at the summit of the Lickey Incline, with an evening local from Birmingham New Street to Worcester in 1960. This locomotive was amongst the last thirty of the class, fitted with side window cabs.
(*John Tarrant*)

already brought about considerable streamlining and modernising of the L.M.S. system, and now it was demanding engines of greater capability than the *Royal Scot* which, for lack of firebox and ashpan capacity, could only make the Euston–Carlisle stretch without stopping.

Of the two initial designs that came quickly off the drawing board, the choice fell on a 4–6–2 with four live steam cylinders and independent valve gear, with 6 ft 6 in. driving wheels. And so in August 1933, the first L.M.S. Pacific proudly took to the rails as No. 6200, named *The Princess Royal*. It was a large engine which without

Left: Not nearly as successful as the 2–6–4 tanks were the seventy Fowler Class 3 2–6–2 tanks of 1930. These engines were underboilered and heartily disliked wherever they went. No. 40051 was recorded outside Nuneaton depot on 18 September 1960, not a noted haunt of the type, which were rendered extinct in 1962. (*John Tarrant*)

tender weighed $104\frac{1}{2}$ tons, and had a tractive effort of just over 40,000 lb. Its front end was reminiscent of the G.W.R. 'Castle'. Further G.W.R. influence was seen in the tapered boiler, and it had a working pressure of 250 lb/in.^{2}. Trials were of course necessary, not only for performance, but for clearance in width for station platforms and height in tunnels and over bridges. This factor had in the past somewhat inhibited the building of large engines with outside cylinders, but tests proved Stanier's contention that this was not a serious handicap. It led to the rapid decision to concentrate on filling a need for many more mixed traffic engines, of

Below: Some of the 'Patriot' 4–6–0s survived in unrebuilt form until withdrawal, unlike the 'Royal Scots' which were all converted. Here is one of the thirty-four un-rebuilt members of the class, No. 45513, standing outside Crewe Works Paint Shop after its last visit there in 1960. The Patriots were used on express passenger services on the LMS system from 1930 until demotion in the early sixties. (*John Warr*)

Above: Ten Fowler docktanks were built in 1928; these outside cylindered 0–6–0s were rare birds, to be seen at such locations as Birkenhead, Liverpool, and Greenock. Here, No. 47165 of Fleetwood is seen just ex Derby Works, at Carnforth in 1961. The locomotives last ran in 1964, 47165 being one of the last two survivors.
(*Allan Preston*)

2–6–0, 2–8–0 and 4–6–0 types. The tapered boiler was adopted also for these, and the 'Stanier' stamp was much in evidence. Even the 'Patriot' Class – the so-called 'Baby Scots' – and the 'Royal Scots' themselves – were later fitted with taper boilers when renewals became necessary. All were, of course, fitted with the now standard Walschaerts valve gear.

Right: Ten 0–4–0 saddle tanks were built for LMS service, five by Kitsons of Leeds in 1932 and five (with greater water capacity) at Horwich in 1953. Care had to be taken to ensure that they didn't run hot when travelling to their place of work. No. 47007 of the later series is shown at Sheep Pasture on the Cromford and High Peak Railway in Derbyshire on 30 September 1961. This mineral line, featuring several rope-worked inclines, is now closed.
(*Derek Smith*)

Left: Only forty of the Stanier 2–6–0s were built; they were an intermediate step between the Hughes 'Crab' and the Stanier 'Black Five', and were usually to be found on the North-Western section of the LMS. Based in the West Midlands was 42957 of Bushbury, here seen shunting at Wolverhampton's Wednesfield Road Goods Yard on 10 October 1964. Built in 1933 and 1934, some of these locomotives survived until 1966. (*Michael Hale*)

It was, however, not until 1934 that Stanier's designs ousted those of his predecessors. Only two of the new 'Princess' Pacifics were built in 1933, and the remaining ten did not appear until 1935. The gap in 1934 was partly due to experiments with the third in line – the 'Turbomotive'. This departure was believed to hold great possibilities in a new field of steam power, but a good deal had to be learned, and by 1935 the decision was reluctantly reached that hopes of breaking away from tradition to achieve more power and reliability at less expense were not likely to be reached. Nor, for that matter, was it felt that the 'Princess' itself was the

Below: *Princess Elizabeth* on parade at the Rail 150 celebrations at Shildon, Co. Durham, on 31 August 1975. The twelve Princess Royal pacifics were built between 1933 and 1935, performing express passenger duties between London Euston, Glasgow, Liverpool and Manchester until their displacement by diesels in the early sixties. No. 6201 was privately preserved after withdrawal in 1962, and entered service hauling enthusiasts specials in 1976. (*D. C. Williams*)

Above: *Princess Elizabeth* in full flight; No. 6201, second of the Princess Royal pacifics, is happily now actively preserved, and is here seen working northwards on the thirteen-coach 'Inter City' railtour at Moreton-on-Lugg, north of Hereford, on 24 April 1976. (*David Stopher*)

final answer, for only ten more were built, whilst during 1934 other smaller Stanier designs emerged – against only eleven of older types.

None of the latter were built in 1935, but a new class of 4–6–0s (of which ninety had been produced in 1934) was proving so successful that another forty came out in 1935. This being King George V's Jubilee year, No. 5552 was named *Silver Jubilee*, and 'Jubilee' became the title of the whole class. They had taper boilers, 6 ft 9 in. driving wheels, and three cylinders, and the engine alone weighed just under 80 tons. They steamed freely, and were very speedy express engines, evoking sufficient pride to receive names indicative of the far-flung British Empire – as well as of the

Right: Another eye-catching exhibition of LMS livery is provided by one of three preserved Jubilee 4–6–0s. Here No. 5690 *Leander*, then housed at Dinting Railway Centre, approaches Malvern tunnel whilst working a special train from Oxford to Hereford in 1974. (*D. C. Williams*)

Royal Navy, and the empire builders. *Bahamas*, *Leander* and *Kolhapur* remain preserved out of the 191 'Jubilees' built.

If some accolade were to be awarded to the most successful British locomotive, it would probably go, not to one of the larger express engines, but to either Gresley's V2 2–6–2 or to Stanier's 4–6–0 'Black Five'. Both were designed for mixed traffic – to be adaptable for both goods and passenger service. And so they were, and 179 L.M.S. 'Black Fives' were built in 1935. It could be said to embody the best of both Great Western and L.M.S. practice, and proved capable not only of competing with

Above: 191 of the Jubilee 4–6–0s were constructed between 1934 and 1936, and after initial troubles with steaming, the class settled down to the effective haulage of express passenger trains over most of the LMS system. At the end of its British Rail career, No. 45593 *Kolhapur* is turned at Carlisle Kingmoor depot during the working of an SLS special on 2 October 1966. Note the pairing with a short 3,500 gallon tender. *Kolhapur* is now preserved at Tyseley, Birmingham. (*Glenn Phillips*)

Left: Evening shadows lengthen as Stanier Class 5 No. 44680 calls at Ruabon whilst working a Stephenson Locomotive Society special from Chester to Birmingham Snow Hill on 5 March 1967. This was the last day of through services from London Paddington to Birkenhead. (*Brian Moone*)

Right: Britain's most successful unconventional steam locomotive was probably No. 6202, unofficially known as the *Turbomotive*. This turbine-driven adaption of the Princess Royal design was introduced in 1935 and operated until 1949, when replacement of parts was considered uneconomical. Rebuilt as a reciprocating locomotive in 1952, No. 46202 *Princess Anne*, was destined to run for only a few months before involvement in the Harrow disaster. Seen in turbine form at Liverpool Edge Hill depot. (*D. J. Montgomery Collection*)

Below: The Stanier Class 5 4–6–0 was probably the most successful steam locomotive in Britain. 842 were built between 1934 and 1951, and they were seen from Bournemouth to Thurso. No. 45312 is just ex-Cowlairs Works, and awaiting delivery to Liverpool Edge Hill depot. The view was taken at Eastfield depot, Glasgow on 27 March 1964.
(*Gavin Morrison*)

the 'Royal Scot' Class for passenger services over almost the whole network, but of hauling heavy goods trains as well. Though the first seventy were subject to slight modification from 1935, building did not cease until 1951, by which time there were no less than 842 in service. All were of two cylinders, giving ample wheel and motion clearance for maintenance, and all had the virtually trouble-free taper boilers. They were amongst the last steam locomotives to give way to diesel, and some fifteen are preserved.

The year 1934 had seen the introduction of more tapered boiler versions of existing

Left: Updating of the Fowler 2–6–4 tank design resulted in both two cylinder and three cylinder Stanier locomotives. Whilst the three cylinder engines were mostly confined to Tilbury line services, the two cylinder engines could be found in most parts of the LMS. No. 42644 puts in a rare appearance amongst the slate tips at Blaenau Ffestiniog, terminus of the Conway Valley branch, on 24 September 1966. British Rail Mark Two coaches were also a rarity at this outpost, forming a Locomotive Club of Great Britain special train. (*Dave Cooke*)

Below: Like their Fowler-designed predecessors, the Stanier Class 3 2–6–2 tanks were sadly underboilered and not liked. Here is No. 40207 outside its home depot, Nuneaton, on 18 September 1960. 139 of these locomotives were built, and four were rebuilt with larger boilers, though proved to be little better. Withdrawals brought an end to the class in 1962. (*John Tarrant*)

L.M.S. locomotives. The first was a three cylinder 2–6–4 tank, and filled the need for something more powerful for the busy London, Tilbury & Southend line. Thirty-seven of these were built, unashamedly L.M.S. despite the eastern location, and they proved so successful that between 1934 and 1939, 186 of them were built for service on the rest of the system. These, however, had only two cylinders. The original L.T.S. three-cylinder tank No. 2500 resides with its forerunner *Thundersley* at Bressingham Museum. A smaller 2–6–2 taper boiler tank was also in production by 1935, following twenty-five 2–6–0 tender engines built in 1934. Both types were modifications of existing parallel boiler designs.

Above: Just as the 'Black Fives' dominated mixed traffic services, so the Stanier 8F 2–8–0s, introduced in 1935, dominated heavy freight work on the LMS system and together with the 4–6–0s, these engines operated until the last days of steam on British Rail in 1968. Many of the 2–8–0s were sent overseas in the Second World War and a maximum of 666 were at work on British Rail. Recently out of Crewe Works, No. 48705 stands in Birmingham New Street Station with an engineers' train on 5 August 1964. The station was in course of rebuilding for electrification at the time. (*John Warr*)

Yet another of Stanier's designs to come off the production line was the 2–8–0 freight locomotive, the engine only weighing 72 tons. This was virtually a 'Black Five' placed on more driving wheels of smaller diameter, giving greater rail adhesion at lower speeds. Even so, it proved capable of over 60 m.p.h. when used in an emergency on passenger work. Although only twenty-one took to the rails in 1935, and only 126 by 1939, it was adopted as a national standard during the war. The Government ordered 240 of them for overseas war service, and building spread to several works other than those of the L.M.S. They were augmented from 1943, as

Right: The last weeks of steam; 8F 2–8–0 No. 48727 of Rose Grove depot heads one of the last steam-hauled 18.35 Preston to Healey Mills freights out of Preston at Farrington Jcn on 1 August 1968. (*Alan Wilkinson*)

Left: The Somerset and Dorset 2–8–0s were only displaced on their own main line by Stanier 8Fs in the final years. Here No. 48706 makes an attractive sight near Midford heading one of the farewell specials before closure of the line, in this case organised somewhat inappropriately by the Great Western Society on 5 March 1966. The tracks are now lifted from this spot; no longer do the Mendip Hills resound to the sounds of hard-worked steam power. Gone, but not forgotten! (*John Chalcraft*)

Right: The high water mark of LMS design under Stanier was reached in 1937 with the Duchess pacifics. No. 6223

a vital link in the war effort, by Riddle's 2–8–0 and 2–10–0 'Austerities', but at their maximum numerical strength 719 of them were running in Britain – including some returned from service overseas. Initially power class 7F, the engines were to become universally known as the '8Fs'.

Despite the halt for a year or two on building of more large express locomotives, the designers and draughtsmen had not been idle. Not all requirements had been met with the 'Princess' Class for more power without running into trouble over excessive weight. The crucial weight factor centred on the axle load, transferred as it was to a very small section of rail at the base of each wheel. The larger boiler to provide more power caused more weight, and the 'Princesses' were rated at 22½ tons per axle. One alternative proposed was to spread extra weight on more axles; a 4–6–4 design came off the drawing board, but its weight was estimated at a total of 187 tons. It was to have a larger boiler, built of lighter-than-normal steel, but though it might well have proved the ultimate in size and strength, it was turned down because of weight and cost. It was estimated that the London–Glasgow run would consume 20,000 gallons of water and 10 tons of coal – equivalent to four shovelfuls per minute for six hours. The L.M.S. were at some disadvantage compared with the L.N.E.R., because their west coast route to Scotland had more severe gradients. But whether or not Stanier was spurred on by news of Gresley's new streamlined Pacifics in the offing, he decided to go ahead with one of his own.

The *Coronation Scot* came out in 1937 – another year of celebration. It was Stanier's answer to Gresley's very successful A4 streamliner, which had achieved 112 m.p.h. with *Silver Link* on its first public run. Stanier's streamlining was impressively modern. On a trial run the locomotive reached 114 m.p.h., and a run from Crewe to Euston was accomplished at only a fraction under 80 m.p.h. – 158 miles in 119 minutes. Its weight (engine only) was 108 tons, with driving wheels 6 ft 9 in. diameter, pressure 250 lb/in.^{2} and a tractive effort of 40,000 lb. The first five engines came out in Prussian Blue livery, though this departure was not adopted as a future standard. The class name 'Coronation' also gave way to 'Duchess', although only ten bore various ducal names, with twenty-one later builds carrying names of cities. Streamlining was dropped because of the difficulties of maintenance and the extra weight of three tons, both of which were not justified by the slightly better performance at higher speeds.

However, the general performance of the new Pacifics came fully up to expectations, and on a trial run No. 6234 *Duchess of Abercorn* recorded the highest sustained power output of any British locomotive. This was of 40,000 lb on Beattock tank, which was an equivalent draw-bar pull of 2,300 h.p. at 30 m.p.h. In retrospect, the late 1930s were the great days of steam. Scarcely anyone realised it at the time, because it was so much a part of everyday life that one expected steam would reign supreme with further developments still to come. Any threat of displacement by diesel or electric had scarcely begun, in spite of the Southern Railways' electrification of their short commuter routes. And if a few unprofitable

Princess Alice of the original blue-and-silver streamlined batch passes Winsford, north of Crewe in 1938.
(*D. J. Montgomery Collection*)

Below: The first ten streamlined engines were followed by five non-streamlined engines: No. 6233 *Duchess of Sutherland* was restored to original condition in 1964, for exhibition at Butlins Holiday Camp, Heads of Ayr. It is seen outside Crewe Works Paint Shop. Built in 1938, No. 6233 was active until 1964 on Anglo-Scottish expresses, a task from which it could rarely be spared until the onset of dieselisation. No. 6233 is now to be seen in steam at Bressingham Gardens. (*Derek Tuck*)

Left: The most improbable location ever devised for a Duchess! No. 46235 *City of Birmingham* sits on the site of the extension to Birmingham's Museum of Science and Industry shortly after the road movement from Landor Street Goods Station on 22 May 1966. The locomotive is exhibited in the condition in which it finally ran for British Railways (except for the dirt). The thirty-eight locomotives of this type were built at Crewe in small quantities from 1937 until 1948, and were withdrawn between 1962 and 1964. Three are preserved. (*Dave Cooke*)

Left: No. 46245 *City of London* is shown in the maroon livery in which sixteen members of the class were repainted from 1959 onwards. This particular engine was a stalwart member of the class, finding employment until the closure of its home depot, Camden, on London Euston to Wolverhampton expresses after most West Coast trains had been dieselised (except for summer Saturday trains and substitution for diesel failures) No. 46245 was photographed leaving Rugby with the 10.16 Birmingham New Street to London Euston on 11 June 1963. (*Derek Smith*)

Left: Some eighteen of the fifty-two Patriot 4–6–0s, or Baby Scots, were officially rebuilt by Stanier from 1946 onwards. 'Officially' because little was left of the original engines; the rebuilds incorporated new taper boilers, new cylinders, and even new cab and tenders. No. 45512 *Bunsen* of Carlisle Upperby stands at Crewe South depot in the era when maintenance was at a low ebb, and these locomotives were mostly in freight service. Mid-1964. (*Allan Preston*)

Above: Rebuilt Royal Scot 4–6–0 No. 46126 finds employment on the 14.30 Camden–Glasgow fitted goods seen at Newbold water troughs, north of Rugby, on 18 October 1962. All seventy-one Royal Scots were rebuilt in a similar manner to the Patriots between 1943 and 1954, but new tenders were not needed and the original cabs were retained. In this form they were a great success, being powerful and steaming well even when consistently overloaded on West Coast route expresses. (*Derek Smith*)

Right: Only one steam design was ascribed to Charles Fairburn; he was principally an electrical engineer. The 2–6–4 tanks introduced from 1945 were updated Stanier engines with shorter wheelbase, and improved maintenance features. Here No. 42277 leaves Wemyss Bay with the 19.50 to Glasgow Central on 2 June 1963. South Clydeside was a favourite haunt of these locomotives. (*David Idle*)

branch lines had been closed already by 1939, and the stock of steam engines of the L.M.S. had fallen from 8,226 in 1933 to 7,664 in 1939, this could have been because of the greater efficiency of those remaining. But war was to have a profound effect.

The L.M.S., along with the other three systems, was placed under Government control two days before war was declared. The railways, as in the 1914–18 war, were required to play a vital part. Troops and evacuees, as well as freight, were a matter of directives against which there could be no argument, and the ordinary passenger services had to take second place along with speed restrictions and staff depletion,

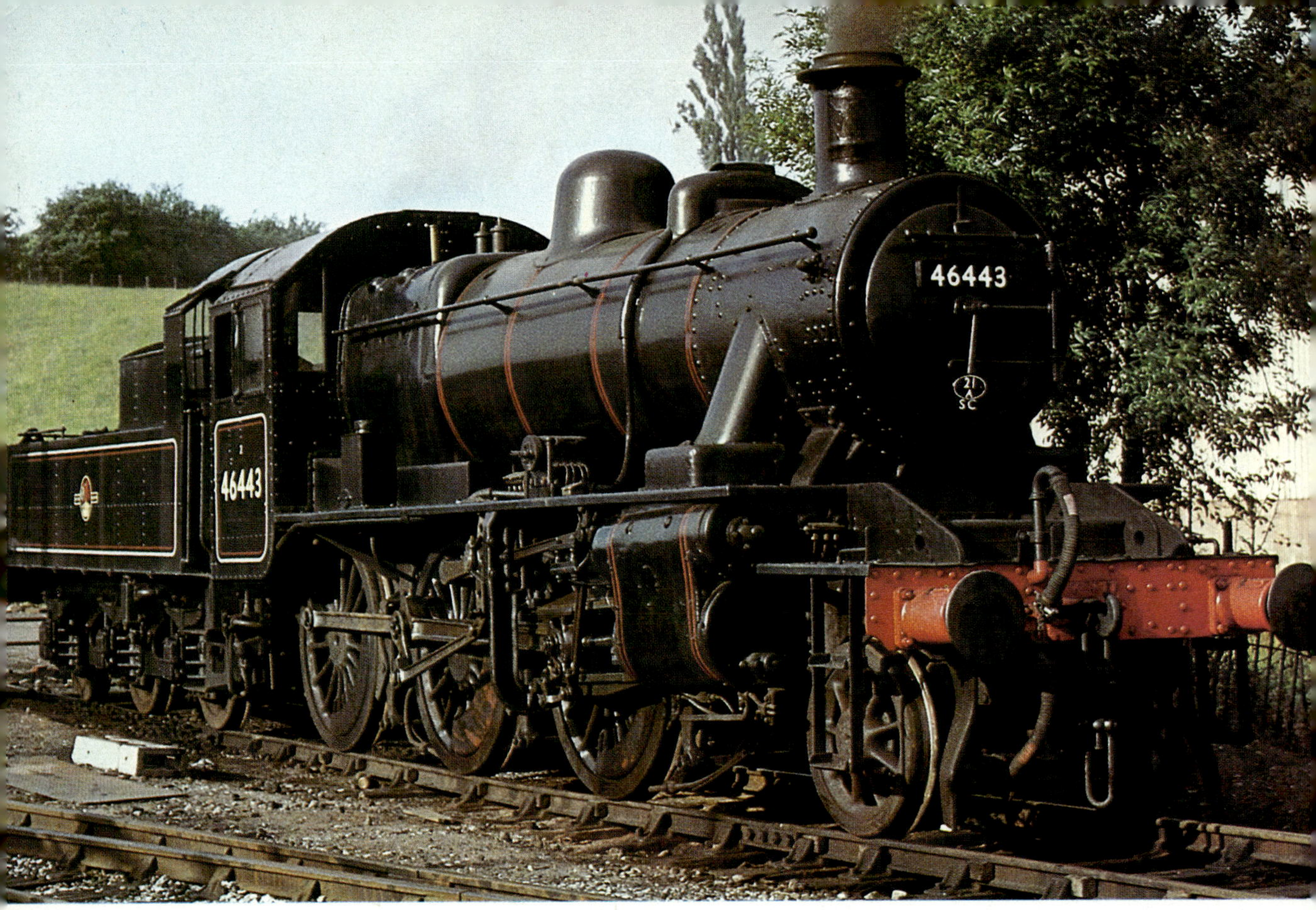
46443
46443

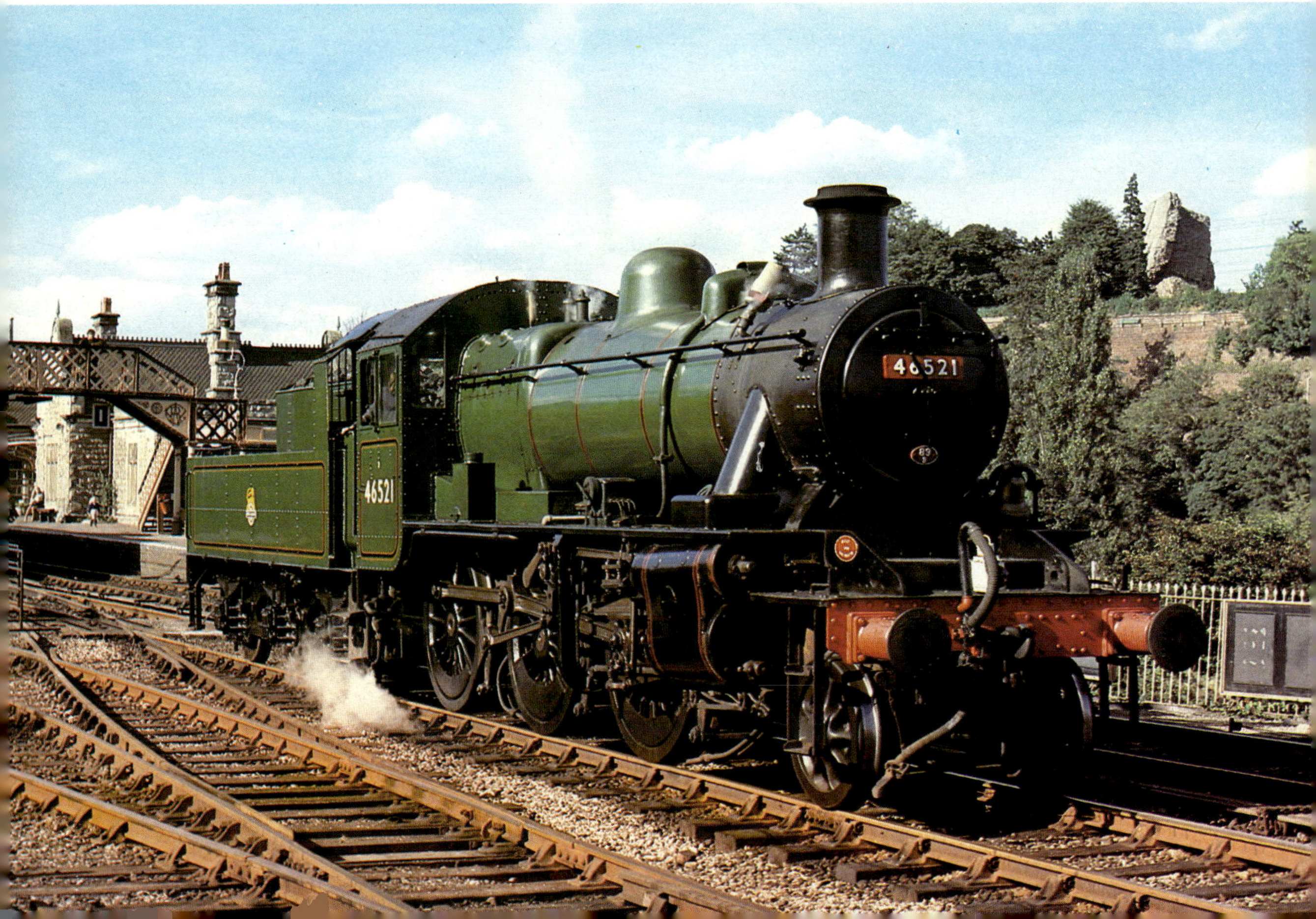
46521
46521

Left: The Ivatt Class 2 2–6–0s, built from 1946 until 1952, heralded a new era in design of light branch line locomotives. No. 46443, built at Crewe in 1950, is here seen at Bridgnorth in 1974. It is regularly used on the Severn Valley Railway. (*D. C. Williams*)

Bottom Left: Some Ivatt 2–6–0s were assembled at Swindon and later sported green livery. No. 46521, formerly at Brecon, has survived six years in a scrapyard to run again. The scene is Bridgnorth on 3 September 1977. (*Bob Green*)

Right: Equally successful was the 2–6–2 tank version particularly on the Southern Region. Here Nos. 41301 and 41284 perform on 'Dorset Belle' railtour duty at Wareham on 27 February 1966. (*Dave Cooke*)

Below: The Ivatt Class 4 2–6–0s, introduced in 1947, were not immediately successful owing to initial poor steaming. The only survivor, No. 43106, at Eardington with the 15.45 Bridgnorth to Bewdley train on 20 April 1976. (*Steve Owen*)

and some railway-works put on war-production schedules. Very few engines indeed were built in the black years of 1940, '41 and '42. From 1943 to 1947, 270 'Black Fives' were built, but only seventeen of the new Pacifics, to add to the twenty built before 1939. That a total of just over 1,000 L.M.S. locomotives were built between 1940 and 1947 was indicative of the requirements for mainly freight and mixed traffic.

Apart from the stress and loss of identity for the L.M.S. during the war, it lost its dynamic overlord, Josiah (Lord) Stamp. His house received a direct hit from a bomb in 1941, killing him, his wife and his son. Sir William Stanier's tenancy of the

key post of C.M.E. came to an end in 1944, after twelve momentous years, though he lived until 1966, aged 88. His place was taken for a short time by C. E. Fairburn, who was only officially credited with one design, being principally an electrical engineer. He produced a modernised 2–6–4 tank, similar to the Stanier type, but with shorter wheelbase. Fairburn died in 1945 and was succeeded by H. G. Ivatt, Stanier's long-standing assistant. He was principally responsible for the introduction of both shunting and main line diesel electric locomotives, but steam was not forgotten in a few important respects. These included some modern aids to maintenance such as the self-cleaning smokebox, hopper ashpan and rocking grate. On big engines such as the 'Duchess' 4–6–2, fire disposal was very hard work, and Ivatt's innovations were popular among enginemen. Ivatt incorporated all these features into three types of locomotive designed for secondary and branch line work. 162 Class 4 2–6–0s were built between 1947 and 1952. In their initial double-chimney form they were unsuccessful, but under B.R. auspices the locomotives proved their worth on passenger and freight. Probably more highly regarded were the Class 2 mixed traffic 2–6–0s and their 2–6–2 tank counterparts, of which over 200 examples were built for light branch line use. These were such good steaming engines that they were universally popular, eventually being used in most parts of Britain. Examples of all these types are preserved, and they have proved very useful on Britain's private lines.

The final stage of development of the Class 5 – the maid of all work – was reached with Ivatt's design, which became the prototype for the B.R. standard types of the 1950s. Steel fireboxes, to save on the cost of copper, were projected, along with some new welding techniques for which Bulleid on the Southern was a pioneer in Britain. Caprotti valve gear was also used, successfully for the first time, and Timken roller bearings – experimental variations which were continued into the B.R. era. 419 new engines, mainly freight and mixed traffic types, were built between the end of 1945 and 1 January 1948; on this date the London Midland & Scottish Railway ceased to exist.

It was indeed the end of an era – a fascinating one for the development of the

Left: Certain experiments were carried out on LMS Class 5 4–6–0s in the late 1940s, involving steel fireboxes, double chimneys, roller bearings and, significantly, types of valve motion. No. 4767 was chosen for the provision of outside Stephenson valve gear, and other features. Though shorn of double blast and electric lighting, the locomotive survived almost to the finale of steam on British Rail. It is here seen leaving Grosmont tunnel with a train for Pickering on the North Yorkshire Moors Railway, on 6 September 1975. (*Bob Green*)
Below: Two 'improved' Duchess pacifics were built under /*see over*

steam locomotive. But if for a few more years steam locomotives remained supreme, a gradually increasing number of factors was telling against them, not least of which were the wasteful use of fuel, and difficulty of finding men to maintain them.

Happily, the L.M.S. is quite well represented in the field of locomotive preservation, a tribute to a large yet well-liked Railway.

WHERE CAN LONDON MIDLAND & SCOTTISH LOCOS STILL BE FOUND?

Large concentrations of active LMS steam locomotives are to be seen on the Severn Valley and Worth Valley Railways. The Severn Valley Railway, from Bridgnorth to Bewdley is actually an ex-GWR line, but half of the locomotives bought to run it are of ex-LMSR origin. The Worth Valley line, joining BR at Keighley, West Yorkshire is a former Midland Railway line. Other places where LMS locomotives pull passenger trains on a regular basis are the North Yorkshire Moors Railway, the Lakeside Railway in Cumbria, the Great Central Railway at Loughborough and the Speyside Railway in the Scottish Highlands.

Ivatt in 1947 and 1948, to bring the total to thirty-eight. No. 46256, named in honour of its designer, stands at Crewe North depot in 1964. These engines had Timken roller bearings, and could be pushed by one man when standing on level track! (*Ken Russell*)

Left: Caprotti valve gear was fitted to twenty Stanier Class 5's by H. G. Ivatt in 1948. These ugly looking machines were not an improvement on the ordinary Class 5's, and a thundering nuisance to maintenance staff in such small quantities. No. 44753 of Holbeck was recorded at Manningham depot, Bradford in 1963, shortly before the locomotive was transferred from the North Eastern to the London Midland Region. (*Allan Preston*)

Below: A scene that delighted train spotters of all ages! Over 100 steam locomotives were 'on shed' at Kingmoor depot, Carlisle, on 2 October 1966. But the end of steam in ordinary British Rail service was less than two years away. (*Glenn Phillips*)

Restored ex-LMSR locomotives are present at the National Railway Museum, York, Butterley (Derbyshire), Bressingham (Norfolk), Carnforth (North Lancashire), Dinting (Near Manchester), Tyseley (Birmingham), Hereford, Cranmore (Somerset) and Glasgow Museum of Transport.

LMS locomotives in course of restoration are stationed at Quainton Road (Buckinghamshire), Southport, Cheddleton (North Staffordshire), Embsay (West Yorkshire), Telford (Salop) and Washford (North Somerset).

Some of the larger locomotives, such as *Princess Elizabeth*, *Scots Guardsman* and *Leander* are seen hauling special trains on the main line of British Rail from time to time, and together with the enthusiast-run branch lines, form a fitting reminder of the great days of London, Midland and Scottish steam.

85306 841 0

Printed by Jarrold & Sons Ltd, Norwich. 280PW